CONTENTS

Some words are printed in bold, **like this**. You can find out what they mean by looking in the glossary.

THE MYSTERIOUS DEEP SEA

In March 2010, a **submarine** was exploring the deep ocean. When it came up to the surface, scientists saw something strange. A bizarre creature was attached to the submarine. The creature looked like a giant crab. It was 76.2 centimetres (2.5 feet) long, from the tip of its head to its tail. The scientists were stunned. They think it latched onto the submarine at a depth of about 2,590 metres (8,497 feet).

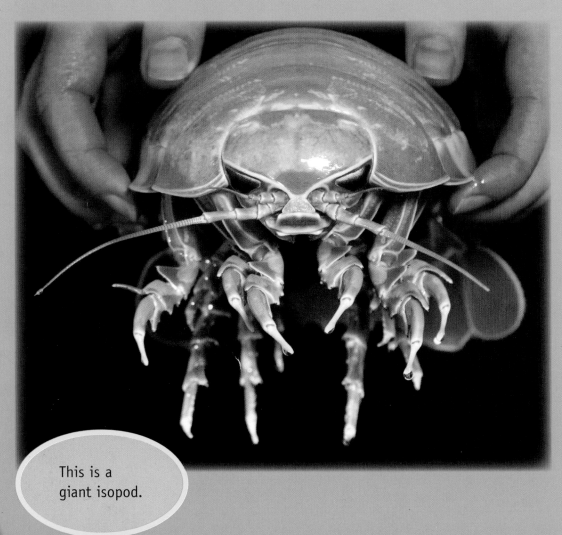

This is a giant isopod.

Ocean Zones

0 metres

200 metres (700 feet)

1000 metres (3,300 feet)

Giant Isopod found at 2,590 metres (8,497 feet)

4,000 metres (13,100 feet)

6,000 metres (19,700 feet)

11,000 metres (36,100 feet)

Sunlight Zone

Twilight Zone

Midnight Zone

Abyssal Zone

Hadal Zone

Earth/rock

Earth/rock

Giant isopods

The creature turned out to be a giant **isopod**. Some people call this creature a "monster bug". It is related to shrimp and crabs. Giant isopods live in the deep waters of the Pacific, Atlantic, and Indian oceans. Scientists know very little about giant isopods. It is difficult to study them in their deep-sea **habitat**. People need special equipment to breathe and move around deep underwater. But giant isopods are amazing creatures!

LIFE IN THE DEEP SEA

Life in the deep sea is difficult. No sunlight makes its way down there. At deep-sea depths, there is total darkness. The water is very cold. There is also intense water **pressure**. The further below the surface, the harder it is to survive.

Monster bugs

Some scary films have featured giant monster bugs. A **crustacean** is not really a bug. But it has many legs like insects do. Giant crustaceans are odd looking creatures. Sometimes people are afraid of things that look strange or unusual.

This is a giant katydid, a type of insect.

A bell jelly glows with bioluminescence.

Glowing creatures

Many deep ocean dwellers have **adapted** to this harsh **habitat.** They have unique features that help them survive there. Some creatures, such as deep-sea shrimp, make their own light. The light is given off after a special reaction takes place. The light produced by living things is called **bioluminescence.** Have you ever seen fireflies at night? They are bioluminescent, too.

Fresh water, salt water

Fresh water is found in lakes and rivers. It contains little salt. Seas and oceans have salt water. The word **marine** is used to describe things from the sea.

DEEP-SEA GIANTS

Some **marine** creatures have unusual features. These features help them survive far below the surface of the water. Features that creatures have developed over time that help them survive are called **adaptations**.

Gigantism

One feature is gigantism. This comes from the word *giant*. Creatures with gigantism are very large. **Crustaceans**, like the giant **isopod**, are more likely to have deep-sea gigantism.

This giant squid weighs 245 kilograms (540 pounds).

Why so large?

So what makes some creatures grow so large? Scientists have a few ideas about this. First, there are fewer **predators** in the deep sea than in other parts of the ocean. Also, animals grow very slowly in such cold water, but have very long lives. The large size helps them control their body temperature.

Smaller creatures

Many creatures in the deep sea are tiny. This makes sense. A small size means a creature does not need much food. It is hard to find food far below the surface. Most deep-sea dwellers feed on dead animals that sink down from above.

This deep-sea amphipod measures a few centimetres.

2.6 centimetres
(1 inch)

CRAFTY CRUSTACEANS

There are many different kinds of **crustaceans**. In fact, there are about 50,000 types! Lobsters, shrimp, water fleas, tiny krill, and copepods are all types of crustacean. Most crustaceans live in the water. Some live in freshwater **habitats**. Others live in **marine** habitats.

Different types of crustacean look very different from one another. But all share one feature: two pairs of **antennae**. They use the antennae for feeling, tasting, and smelling. Insects only have one pair of antennae.

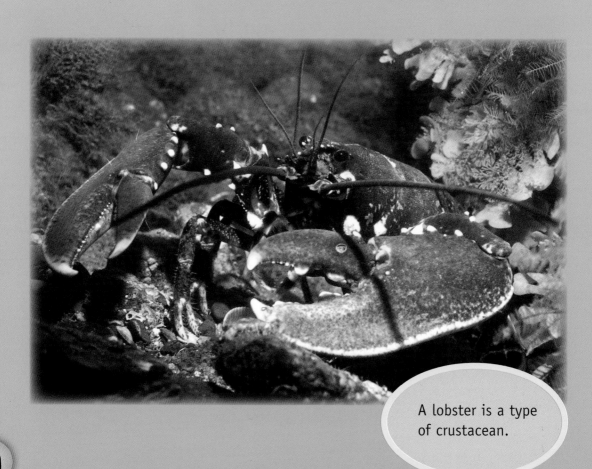

A lobster is a type of crustacean.

Skeleton on the outside?

All crustaceans have an **exoskeleton**. An exoskeleton is a hard covering on the outside of the body. This hard covering supports and holds in the crustacean's body. (A human skeleton is on the inside.) When a crustacean grows, it moults. This means it sheds its exoskeleton. But don't worry! It grows another, larger one.

A ghost crab, a type of scavenger, feeds on a dead fish.

Finding food

Most crustaceans are **scavengers**. They feed on dead plants and animals. Some are **predators**. That means they hunt other animals for food.

MARINE ISOPODS

Marine isopods are a type of **crustacean**. The word *isopod* means "equal-footed". Marine isopods are many-legged creatures that live in the water. Most live on or near the seafloor.

Sea slater

A common type of isopod is the sea slater. It lives under stones and in cracks in rocks. Fully grown, it has seven pairs of legs. Sea slaters hide during the day. At night they come out and feed on brown seaweed.

Can you count how many pairs of legs this sea slater has?

Yuck!

One unusual isopod is a type of louse. It replaces the tongue of certain fish! First, it sneaks in through the fish's gills. Then it attaches to and eats away at the tongue. This tongue-eating louse will latch onto what's left of the tongue and continue to live in the fish's mouth. The fish lives on and can still eat.

Roly-poly relatives

Aquatic isopods are related to the woodlouse. Some people call this a roly-poly. They can roll into a ball for self-defence. Curved into a ball, their hard **exoskeleton** protects them.

This grey garden woodlouse lives in the soil.

GIANT ISOPODS

Giant **isopods** are the largest **aquatic** isopods. They live in the deep waters of all the oceans. Giant isopods are found 170 to 2,140 metres (550 to 7,020 feet) below the surface of the water. They grow up to 46 centimetres (18 inches) long.

What's for dinner?

Giant isopods are **scavengers**. This means they feed on dead animals. Giant isopods feed on the carcasses of whales and fish. This dead matter sinks down to the sea floor from above. The giant isopod's complex mouth helps it to tear its food apart. Some scientists believe the giant isopod also feeds on live **sponges** and **sea cucumbers**.

Giant isopods feed on the remains of dead fish, such as this shark.

Do people eat giant isopods?

It is difficult to fish for giant isopods. They live far below the surface of the water. Fishermen don't cast their nets and traps that deep. By the time the giant isopod reaches the surface, it has been scavenged by other creatures. But occasionally fishermen catch a giant isopod that reaches the surface intact. It is then sold in markets and eaten in some parts of the world.

These giant isopods have been accidentally caught by fishermen.

GIANT EGGS AND ROLY-POLIES

Scientists first discovered the giant **isopod** over 130 years ago. But they know very little about how giant isopods live. It is difficult to study them in their **habitat**. The deep sea is very dark and cold. People cannot survive that far underwater without special equipment.

Giant isopods have the largest eggs of any **marine invertebrate**. Invertebrates are animals without a backbone. (Humans have backbones. **Crustaceans** do not. They have **exoskeletons**.) Mother giant isopods **brood** their eggs under plates on their legs.

The giant isopod is found thousands of metres below the surface of the ocean. This makes it difficult for scientists to study them.

Protection from attack

When it is attacked, a giant isopod can roll itself into a ball. This is just like the woodlouse, or roly-poly. The hard exoskeleton protects the giant isopod from **predators**.

Scientists

Alphonse Milne-Edwards was a French scientist. He lived from 1835 to 1900. He discovered the giant isopod in 1879. He fished a huge male isopod out of the Gulf of Mexico. People were excited about this amazing discovery. And they still are!

A woodlouse rolls into a ball to protect itself from a predator, just like a giant isopod.

BOILED SHRIMP

Another type of crafty **crustacean** lives in the deep sea – shrimp. These deep-sea shrimp are very different from the shrimp you eat.

Surviving the heat

Some kinds of shrimp can survive very harsh conditions. They are found near vents that let out hot steam and liquids from deep within Earth. Temperatures near these vents are very high. The water may be boiling hot – or even hotter. In some places, the water is hot enough to melt lead!

Deep-sea shrimp cluster near a vent.

Adaptations

Other shrimp can deal with extreme cold. Some of these shrimp have very large eyes. This helps them take in what little light there is in the deep sea. Other shrimp are **bioluminescent**. They make their own light. This helps them to distract or blind **predators**.

This deep-sea shrimp has bioluminescent organs.

WOOD-EATING CRABS

Some types of crabs have also developed unusual features. These features helped them **adapt** to their deep-sea **habitat**.

One type of crab has very odd eating habits. Wood-eating crabs munch on trees and other pieces of wood that have fallen to the ocean floor. They even feast on shipwrecks! Scientists found out about their strange diet by cutting a dead crab open. They looked at the contents of its stomach. Inside its stomach was shredded wood!

This crafty crustacean is a wood-eating crab.

Different eating habits

Eating wood is a strange behaviour for a crab. Most **crustaceans** are **scavengers**. They eat dead animal matter that floats down from above. Other crustaceans are **predators**. They feed on other animals. But these wood-eating crabs only eat plant matter. Their stomachs contain **bacteria** that help them to break down wood.

Crab or lobster?

Another name for the wood-eating crab is the squat lobster. But it is not a lobster at all. It is a type of crab.

This squat lobster makes its home near a vent.

BLIND LOBSTERS, FURRY LOBSTERS

Two types of lobsters have developed very strange features. These features helped them **adapt** to life in the deep ocean.

Claws to help see

Blind lobsters cannot see. Eyes are not much help so deep below the water's surface. Little or no sunlight filters down that far. Instead, blind lobsters have very long, thin claws. They look a bit like tweezers. The claws help them find and capture food. They also help the lobsters move around on the sea floor.

The blind lobster uses its claws, not eyes, to find food.

The furry lobster is an eyeless crustacean.

A fur coat for protection

Another type of **crustacean** lives in the deep ocean. The furry crustacean has a white body covered with long, hair-like strands. It lives very deep in the ocean, at about 2,300 metres (7,546 feet). The furry crustacean lives near **hydrothermal** vents. These hot vents spew out (release) steam and poisons. **Bacteria** in the crustacean's fur help it to filter out poisons. This helps it survive in its harsh **habitat**. Like the blind crustaceans, furry crustaceans cannot see either. There is no light deep in the sea where they live.

EXPLORING THE DEEP SEA

Crafty **crustaceans** have **adapted** to life in the deep ocean. Humans have not. We cannot survive for long in the deep sea. The extreme cold and **pressure** are deadly to humans.

But there are many reasons to explore the deep sea. Scientists want to learn about the amazing animals that live there. But they cannot just swim down and look around. Even a wet suit and scuba gear are not enough. To explore the deep ocean, scientists need special vehicles and equipment.

This remote viewer studies a deep-sea crab.

Scientists

Many scientists study the deep sea. **Marine biologists** focus on ocean-dwelling animals.

This early deep-sea vehicle, called a bathysphere, helped scienctists explore the deep ocean.

The bathysphere

One early deep-sea device was the bathysphere. It was a round **sphere** made of steel. Two people could fit inside. The steel withstood the intense water pressure. Inside was an oxygen tank so the people could breathe. In 1934 two scientists dived down to 923 metres (3,028 feet) below the surface. At the time, no one had been that far underwater.

COOL TOOLS

Deep-sea devices have come a long way since the bathysphere. Today there are many cool tools that help scientists explore the ocean floor.

Small submarines

Deep-sea **submersibles** travel far underwater. They are like **submarines**, only smaller. Some submersibles stay attached to boats or submarines on the surface. Scientists fit inside and control the movement of the submersible. They explore the deep ocean and collect animal samples. Giant isopods move too fast for submersibles to catch. But they can be caught in traps.

Vehicles like this help scientists explore the deep ocean.

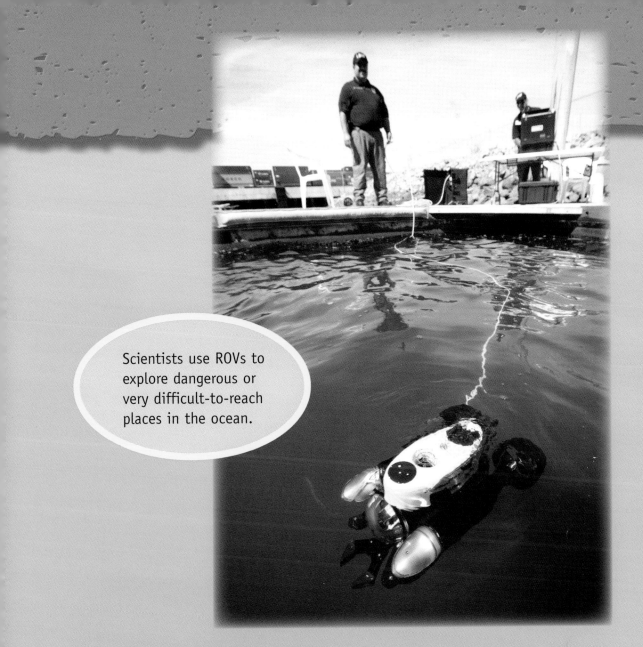

Scientists use ROVs to explore dangerous or very difficult-to-reach places in the ocean.

Remote control

Other tools are controlled from above. These are called ROVs, short for "remotely operated vehicles". These submarine robots move around the ocean floor, take pictures or videos, and collect samples. ROVs can get to places that are too dangerous for humans.

SAVING THE DEEP SEA

The world's oceans are so large, it may seem like we do not need to worry about them. But we do.

Danger from people

The deep ocean is Earth's largest habitat. Today this unique habitat is in danger. **Pollution** threatens to change or harm the deep sea. Human activity has led to **global warming**. Slowly, the temperatures in the deep sea are rising. Crustaceans and other animals that are used to very cold conditions may not survive. They cannot **adapt** quickly enough to these changes.

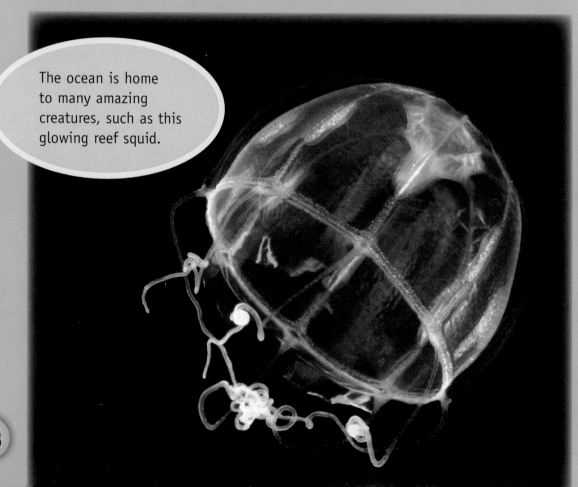

The ocean is home to many amazing creatures, such as this glowing reef squid.

Pollution, such as the oil shown here, is a serious threat to the world's oceans.

More to explore

It is important to protect the deep ocean. There is still a lot to learn about it. We know very little about many of the amazing animals that live there. Many deep-sea dwellers have not been discovered yet. Scientists know more about the surface of the moon than the deep sea.

Final frontier

Very few people have explored the deep sea. In fact, more people have gone into space!

GLOSSARY

adapt change to fit an environment

adaptation feature developed over time that helps a living thing to survive in its environment

antenna (plural: antennae) sense organ on the head

aquatic having to do with water

bacteria single-celled living things that can only be seen under a microscope

bioluminescence light given off by a living thing

brood grow eggs

crustacean type of living thing with a hard exoskeleton, two pairs of antennae, and a pair of legs on each segment

exoskeleton hard outer structure on some animals

global warming rise in temperature that is taking place around the world

habitat place where a living thing lives

hydrothermal having to do with hot water

invertebrate animal without a backbone

isopod group of marine crustaceans

marine having to do with the ocean

marine biologist scientist who studies plants and animals in the ocean

pollution harmful waste

predator animal that hunts other animals

pressure weight or force that pushes against something

scavenger animal that eats dead plant or animal matter

sea cucumber simple marine invertebrate with a cucumber-shaped body

sphere evenly round object like a ball

sponge simple marine invertebrate with a soft body

submarine vehicle built to operate underwater

submersible small underwater craft

FIND OUT MORE

Books

Deep Oceans (Earth's Final Frontiers), Anna Claybourne (Heinemann Library, 2008)

Ocean (DK Eyewitness Books), Miranda MacQuitty (Dorling Kindersley, 2008)

The Deep, Deep Ocean (Oceans Alive!), John Woodward (Franklin Watts, 2009)

Websites

news.bbc.co.uk/earth/hi/earth_news/newsid_ 8638000/8638527.stm
Watch this remarkable film captured by scientists using a remotely operated vehicle (ROV).

news.bbc.co.uk/1/hi/world/europe/jersey/ 8246001.stm
Find out more about the crafty tongue-eating isopod.

www.bbc.co.uk/nature/habitats/Hydrothermal_vent
Find out more about hydrothermal vents and the creatures that live near them.

INDEX